SECOND SERIES

More Classics to Moderns

Compiled and edited by Denes Agay

It is with pleasure that we present More Classics To Moderns. It is a sequel to our now widely used Classics To Moderns.

Because of the extended period of music history in both books, beginning pianists of all ages will discover material well suited to their needs. This material is easy enough to be used by the beginning student as his first sight reading book. At the university level, the student will find a rich source of reference to supplement his study of theory and composition.

The original compositions selected by Denes Agay involved extensive research covering the piano literature of more than three centuries. There is a wide representation of composers, including some of the lesser known masters, all of whom the player will be delighted to encounter.

All selections are in their original form, neither re-arranged nor simplified. They appear in approximately chronological order. Marks of phrasing and expression are often editorial additions, especially in the music of the pre-classic period. These signs were added for a quicker and easier understanding of the structure and mood of the compositions. They are to be considered as suggestions rather than rigid directions.

Students, teachers and all pianists will find these original miniatures valuable for study, recital, sight reading or just relaxing musical entertainment of the highest calibre. *The Publishers*

Yorktown Music Press

London/New York/Sydney

Exclusive Distributors:
Music Sales Limited
8/9 Frith Street, London W1V 5TZ, England
Music Sales Corporation
257 Park Avenue South, New York, NY10010, USA
Music Sales Pty. Limited
120 Rothschild Avenue, Rosebery, NSW 2018, Australia

This book © Copyright 1979 by
Yorktown Music Press
ISBN 0.86001.678.1
Order No. YK 20139

Music Sales complete catalogue lists thousands of titles
and is free from your local music book shop, or direct from
Music Sales Limited. Please send a cheque/postal order
for £1.50 for postage to
Music Sales Limited, 8/9 Frith Street, London W1V 5TZ

CONTENTS

Minuet

Henry Purcell
(1659-1695)

Rigaudon

St. Catherine

John Barrett
(1674–1735)

* *Inner voices may be omitted.*

© 1979 Yorktown Music Press, Inc.

Danse Galante

Georg Philipp Telemann
(1681–1767)

Minuet

Johann Sebastian Bach
(1685-1750)

Rondino

Jean Philippe Rameau
(1683-1764)

Gavotte

George Frideric Handel
(1685-1759)

Little Serenade

German Dance

Joseph Haydn
(1732-1809)

Gypsy Dance

Allegro moderato

Joseph Haydn

Minuet

(K.315a)

Wolfgang Amadeus Mozart
(1756–1791)

Spring Song

(K.596)*

Allegretto giocoso

Wolfgang Amadeus Mozart

mf

legato sempre

* *Original piano part of the song, "Come Sweet May."*

© Copyright 1965 Yorktown Music Press, Inc.

German Dance

Ludwig van Beethoven
(1770-1827)

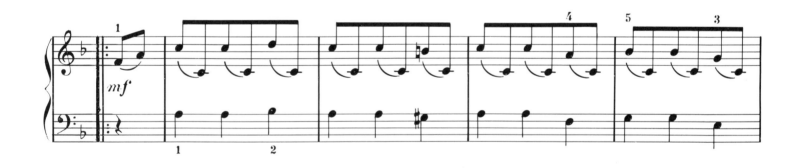

Bagatelle

Antonio Diabelli
(1781–1858)

Ländler

Franz Schubert
(1797-1828)

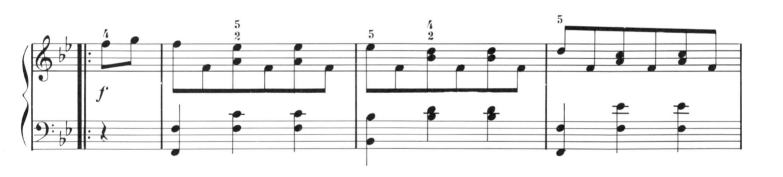

Two Ecossaises

1.

Friedrich Kuhlau
(1786–1832)

2.

The Dancing Master

Daniel Gottlob Türk
(1756–1813)

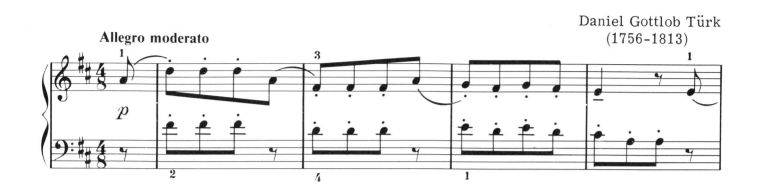

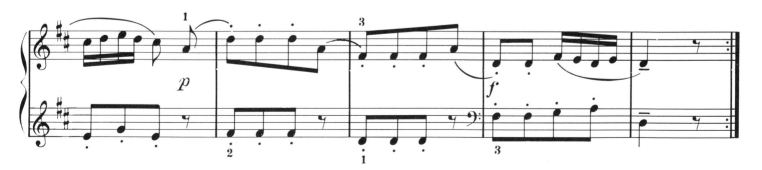

Merry Farmer Returning From Work

(Op.68, No.10)

Robert Schumann
(1810-1856)

Playful Dialogue

Johann Nepomuk Hummel
(1778–1837)

Scherzo
(Op.55, No.1)

Ignaz Moscheles
(1794–1870)

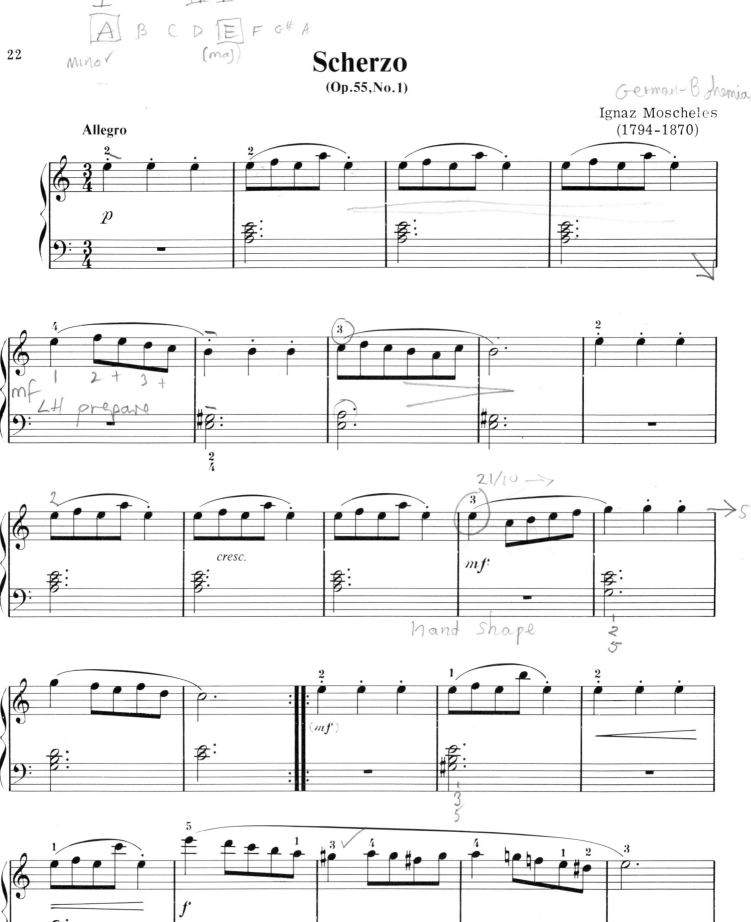

The Doll's Funeral March
(Op.39, No.7)

Peter Ilyich Tchaikovsky
(1840-1893)

The Shepherd's Flute

Samuel Maykapar
(1867–1938)

Dance With Me

(from Op.27)

Robert Volkmann
(1815–1883)

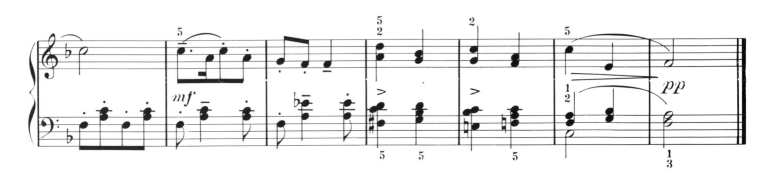

The Chinese Doll

Vladimir Rebikoff
(1866-1920)

Scherzino

Aram Khatchaturian
(1903-   )

Pastorale

Elena Gnessina

Dainty Ballerina

Op.27, No.6

Dmitri Kabalevsky
(1906-   )

The Hobby Horse
(Op.39, No.15)

Dmitri Kabalevsky
(1904-   )

Sonatina

Allegro moderato

T. Salutrinskaya

Printed in the United Kingdom by Printwise (Haverhill) Limited, Haverhill, Suffolk   8/99 (35029)